Gooseberry Patch Co.

Our Favorite
Slow-Cooker
Chicken & Beef Recipes

Copyright 2008, Gooseberry Patch
Third Printing, July, 2011

Slow cookers are ideal for any country supper potluck.
Tote them filled with your favorite spiced cider, shredded
chicken, hearty stew or cobbler...scrumptious!

2

Hearty Chick'n Dumplings

Makes 4 servings

2 10-3/4 oz. cans cream of
  chicken soup
2 14-1/2 oz. cans chicken broth
1/2 onion, diced

1 lb. boneless, skinless chicken
  breasts
2 6.3-oz. tubes refrigerated
  biscuits, quartered

Combine first 3 ingredients in a slow cooker. Add chicken; cover and cook on high setting for 4 to 5 hours. During the last hour of cooking, remove chicken and shred with 2 forks; return to slow cooker. Add biscuit pieces to chicken mixture; stir to coat. Cover and cook on high setting for one hour.

Good gravy...it's easy! Remove the cooked meat from the slow
cooker, leaving juices inside. Make a smooth paste of 1/4 cup
cold water and 1/4 cup cornstarch. Pour into the slow cooker,
stir well and turn to high setting. Cook for 15 minutes once
the mixture comes to a boil. Stir again before serving.

Country Chicken Dinner

Makes 4 to 6 servings

3 c. potatoes, peeled and cubed
3 c. baby carrots
1 onion, coarsely chopped
4 chicken breasts, halved
1 c. water
2 .87-oz. pkgs. chicken gravy
   mix

1 t. seasoned salt
1 t. dried thyme
1/4 t. poultry seasoning
1 c. sour cream

Place potatoes, carrots and onion in a slow cooker. Arrange chicken on top, overlapping slightly; set aside. Combine water, gravy mix and seasonings in a small bowl; drizzle over chicken. Cover and cook on low setting for 8 hours, or on high setting for 4 hours. Remove chicken and vegetables to a serving platter. Whisk sour cream into drippings in slow cooker; pour over chicken and vegetables.

Try spooning any favorite sandwich fillings
into a pita pocket...less mess!

Zesty Chicken Sandwiches

Makes 4 servings

4 boneless, skinless chicken
   breasts
1-1/2 oz. pkg. onion soup mix
1/4 t. garlic salt
1/4 c. Italian salad dressing

1/4 c. water
4 sandwich buns, split
Garnish: lettuce, sliced cheese,
   sour cream or ranch salad
   dressing

Place chicken in a slow cooker; sprinkle with soup mix and garlic salt.
Drizzle dressing and water over chicken. Cover and cook on low
setting for 8 to 9 hours. Remove chicken and shred with 2 forks;
return to slow cooker. Serve with a slotted spoon on buns; garnish
as desired.

Resist the urge to lift the lid of your slow cooker to take a peek!
Lifting the lid lets out the heat and makes cooking time longer.

Savory Chicken Soup

Makes 4 to 6 servings

2 carrots, peeled and sliced
2 stalks celery, chopped
2 to 3 potatoes, peeled and
    quartered
Optional: 2 onions, sliced
3 boneless, skinless chicken
    breasts, cubed

14-1/2 oz. can chicken broth
2 c. water
1/4 t. salt
1/4 t. pepper
1/2 t. dried parsley
1/2 t. dried basil

Place all vegetables in a slow cooker; add chicken. Pour in broth and water; sprinkle seasonings over top. Cover and cook on low setting for 8 hours, or on high setting for 4 hours. Serves 4 to 6.

A toasty touch for soups! Butter bread slices and cut into shapes using mini cookie cutters. Heat on a baking sheet at 425 degrees until crisp and then garnish filled soup bowls before serving.

Chicken Corn Chowder

Makes 8 to 10 servings

2 T. butter
2 boneless, skinless chicken
    breasts, diced
2 onions, chopped
2 stalks celery, sliced
16-oz. pkg. baby carrots,
    halved
4 c. frozen corn, thawed

4 10-3/4 oz. cans cream of
    potato soup
3 c. chicken broth
1 t. dill weed
1 c. half-and-half
Optional: croutons, additional
    dill weed

Melt butter in a skillet over medium heat; cook chicken until golden.
Combine chicken and remaining ingredients except half-and-half and
garnish in a slow cooker. Cover and cook on high setting for 4 hours,
until carrots are tender. Turn slow cooker off; stir in half-and-half.
Let stand for 5 to 10 minutes, until warmed through. Garnish with
croutons and a sprinkle of dill weed, if desired.

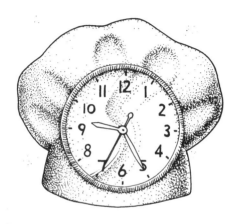

Some foods taste even better the second day. Slow-cook overnight, then in the morning, cool and spoon into a food storage container to refrigerate. At dinnertime, reheat on the stovetop until piping hot...mmm!

Chicken Italiano

Makes 4 to 6 servings

14-1/2 oz. can diced tomatoes, drained
7-oz. can sliced mushrooms, drained
2-1/2 oz. can sliced black olives, drained
1/2 c. onion, chopped
1/2 c. green pepper, diced
3 T. tomato paste
2 T. capers

2 T. olive oil
1 T. garlic, minced
1/2 t. salt
1 t. pepper
1/2 t. dried oregano
Optional: 2 T. red wine
2 lbs. boneless, skinless chicken thighs
cooked thin spaghetti

Combine all ingredients except chicken and spaghetti in a slow cooker; mix well. Add chicken and stir to coat. Cover and cook on low setting for 8 hours. Serve over hot, cooked spaghetti.

☑ chicken breasts
☑ chicken broth
☑ cream of mushroom soup
☑ sliced mushrooms

There are so many great-tasting cream soups...mushroom, celery, onion and chicken. Shake up a favorite recipe by trying a different one each time!

Creamy Mushroom Chicken   *Makes 4 to 6 servings*

1 lb. boneless, skinless chicken
    breasts, cubed
1-1/4 oz. pkg. chicken gravy
    mix
10-3/4 oz. can cream of
    mushroom soup

1 c. white wine or chicken broth
8-oz. pkg. cream cheese, cubed
cooked pasta or rice

Place chicken in a slow cooker. Sprinkle gravy mix over chicken; add soup and wine or broth. Cover and cook on low setting for 5 to 6 hours. Add cream cheese 30 minutes before serving. Remove chicken from slow cooker; vigorously whisk sauce. Serve chicken and sauce over hot, cooked pasta or rice.

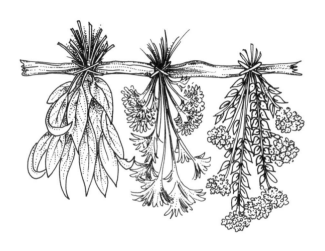

Herbs from your garden will look (and smell!) wonderful hanging from peg boards, ready to add snips to favorite recipes. Rosemary, tarragon and thyme are especially good with chicken.

California Chicken Casserole *Makes 4 to 6 servings*

1/2 c. butter, diced
16-oz. pkg. frozen mixed
   vegetables, thawed
2 10-3/4 oz. cans cream of
   chicken soup
2 10-3/4 oz. cans cream of
   mushroom soup

1 T. garlic powder
1 T. onion powder
3 3-oz. pkgs. chicken-flavored
   ramen noodles
6 boneless, skinless chicken
   breasts, cut into bite-size
   pieces

Place butter in a slow cooker. Add vegetables and soups; mix well.
Sprinkle with garlic powder, onion powder and seasoning packets
from ramen noodles. Arrange chicken on top. Cover and cook on low
setting for 6 hours. Break ramen noodles into quarters; add to slow
cooker. Stir to cover noodles. Cover and cook on high setting for one
hour, until noodles are tender.

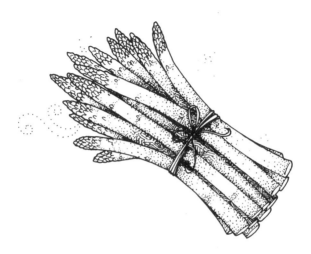

Asparagus makes such an elegant side dish and is surprisingly simple to prepare! Simply place the spears on a sheet of aluminum foil, drizzle with olive oil and sprinkle with garlic salt. Broil for about 5 minutes, or until tender.

Charlene's Ritzy Chicken

Makes 4 to 6 servings

10-3/4 oz. can cream of chicken
    soup
2 c. sour cream
1 sleeve round buttery crackers,
    crushed

1/2 c. butter, melted
4 to 6 boneless, skinless
    chicken breasts
mashed potatoes

Combine soup and sour cream in a small bowl; set aside. In a separate bowl, mix together crackers and butter. Place chicken in a slow cooker; spoon soup mixture over top and sprinkle with cracker mixture. Cover and cook on low setting for 7 to 9 hours, or on high setting for 4 to 5 hours. Serve over mashed potatoes.

A hearty dish like Down-Home Chicken & Noodles is perfect on a cool autumn night. Carry the crock right out to your backyard picnic table and savor the fall colors with your family!

Down-Home Chicken & Noodles

Makes 6 servings

1 lb. boneless, skinless chicken
   breasts
salt and pepper to taste
2 10-3/4 oz. cans cream of
   chicken soup

14-1/2 oz. can chicken broth
16-oz. pkg. wide egg noodles,
   cooked

Place chicken in a slow cooker; sprinkle with salt and pepper. Top
with soup. Cover and cook on low setting for 6 hours, or until chicken
falls apart. Remove chicken from slow cooker and shred. Return
chicken to slow cooker; add broth and cooked noodles. Mix well.
Cover and cook on low setting for an additional 30 minutes, or until
heated through.

Barbecue is delicious...and gooey! If the party is outside,
be sure to bring along some moist towelettes or
napkins to clean up sticky little hands and faces.

Aunt Jo's BBQ

Makes 6 servings

4 lbs. chicken
4 t. mustard
4 t. chili powder

2 t. pepper
1 c. vinegar

Place chicken in a slow cooker. Combine remaining ingredients; pour over chicken. Cover and cook on low setting for 6 to 8 hours, or on high setting for 3 to 4 hours.

Simple slow-cooker recipes are ideal for older children just
learning to cook. With supervision, they can learn to use
paring knives, can openers and hot mitts...and they'll be
oh-so-proud to serve the dinner they've prepared!

4-Ingredient Chicken Chili   *Makes 4 to 6 servings*

4 boneless, skinless chicken
   breasts
8-oz. pkg. Monterey Jack
   cheese, cubed

16-oz. jar salsa
3 15-1/2 oz. cans Great
   Northern beans, drained
   and rinsed

Cover chicken breasts with water in a saucepan; simmer until cooked
through, about 20 to 30 minutes. Reserve broth and shred chicken.
Add reserved broth and chicken to a slow cooker; stir in cheese. Add
salsa and beans to chicken mixture. Cover and cook on low setting for
one to 2 hours, or until heated through and cheese is melted.

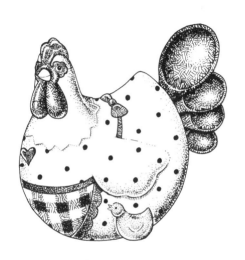

Soups taste even better the next day...why not make a double batch? Let it cool thoroughly, then cover and refrigerate for up to 3 days. Supper tonight, an easy lunch later on.

Chicken & Broccoli Chowder   *Makes 4 to 6 servings*

1 lb. boneless, skinless chicken
   thighs, cubed
14-1/2 oz. can chicken broth
1/2 c. water
1 c. baby carrots, sliced
1 c. sliced mushrooms
1/2 c. onion, chopped
1/4 t. garlic powder

1/8 t. dried thyme
10-3/4 oz. can cream of chicken
   & broccoli soup
1/2 c. milk
3 T. all-purpose flour
10-oz. pkg. frozen broccoli,
   thawed

Combine chicken, broth, water, carrots, mushrooms, onion and
seasonings in a slow cooker; mix well. Cover and cook on low setting
for 7 to 9 hours. In a small bowl, whisk together soup, milk and
flour; stir into slow cooker along with broccoli. Cover and cook an
additional 30 minutes, or until heated through and broccoli is tender.

It's best to thaw meat before slow cooking, if possible. Otherwise, cook on high for the first hour, then reduce to low and cook as usual...ingredients will rise quickly to a safe temperature.

Cranberry Chicken

Makes 6 to 8 servings

3 to 4 lbs. chicken
16-oz. can whole-berry
   cranberry sauce
1 c. barbecue sauce

1/2 c. celery, diced
1/2 c. onion, diced
1/2 t. salt
1/4 t. pepper

Combine all ingredients in a slow cooker. Cover and cook on low setting for 6 to 8 hours, or on high setting for 4 hours.

Don't worry about slow-cooking temperatures being below what's considered safe for chicken. The Low setting is about 200 degrees, while the High setting is about 300 degrees... both are well above the safe temperature of 140 degrees.

Autumn Nutmeg Chicken

Makes 6 servings

6 boneless, skinless chicken
  breast halves
1 to 2 T. oil
1 onion, chopped
1/4 c. fresh parsley, minced
2 10-3/4 oz. cans cream of
  mushroom soup

1/2 c. sour cream
1/2 c. milk
1 T. nutmeg
1/4 t. dried rosemary
1/4 t. dried sage
1/4 t. dried thyme
cooked rice

In a skillet over medium heat, brown chicken in oil; reserve drippings. Arrange chicken in a slow cooker; set aside. Sauté onion and parsley in reserved drippings until onion is tender. Add remaining ingredients except rice; mix well and pour over chicken. Cover and cook on low setting for 5 hours, or until juices run clear when chicken is pierced. Serve over cooked rice.

To keep rice from becoming sticky, don't stir it after cooking,
instead, gently fluff it with a fork. It works every time!

Mom's Company Chicken

Makes 6 servings

2 lbs. boneless, skinless
    chicken thighs
3 cloves garlic, minced
1 onion, chopped

1/2 c. sweet-and-sour sauce
1/2 c. barbecue sauce
cooked rice or couscous

Combine all ingredients except rice or couscous in a slow cooker.
Cover and cook on low setting for 8 to 9 hours, until chicken is
cooked through. Serve over cooked rice or couscous.

Plug your slow cooker into an automatic timer if you need it to start
cooking while you're away from home. Well-chilled foods can
safely be held at room temperature for one to 2 hours.

Mozzarella Chicken & Rice

Makes 8 servings

8 boneless, skinless chicken
   breasts
1/4 t. salt
1/8 t. pepper
1 onion, chopped

2 green peppers, coarsely
   chopped
2 c. pasta sauce
1 c. shredded mozzarella cheese
cooked orzo pasta or rice

Place chicken in a slow cooker; sprinkle with salt and pepper. Top
with onion and green peppers; pour pasta sauce over top. Cover
and cook on low setting for 4 to 5 hours. Stir well and sprinkle with
cheese. Let stand for 5 minutes, until cheese is melted. Serve over
cooked pasta or rice.

Dress up the table in south-of-the-border style when serving Fiesta Chicken Pronto...arrange colorful woven blankets, sombreros and tissue paper flowers around the room!

Fiesta Chicken Pronto

Makes 8 servings

8 boneless, skinless chicken
   breasts
16-oz. can black beans, drained
   and rinsed

10-3/4 oz. can cream of chicken
   soup
2 T. taco seasoning mix
1/4 c. salsa

Arrange chicken in a slow cooker. Combine remaining ingredients and pour over chicken. Cover and cook on low setting for 6 to 7 hours, or on high setting for 3 hours.

To shred cooked chicken, use two forks and insert the prongs, back sides facing each other, into the center of a portion of meat. Then simply pull the forks gently away from each other.

Anne's Chicken Burritos

Makes 6 to 8 servings

6 boneless, skinless chicken
   breasts
15-1/4 oz. can corn, drained
16-oz. can black beans, drained
   and rinsed

16-oz. jar salsa
6 to 8 10-inch flour tortillas
Garnish: shredded Cheddar
   cheese, sour cream, salsa

Combine chicken, corn, beans and salsa in a slow cooker. Cover and cook on low setting for 8 to 10 hours, or on high setting for 4 to 6 hours. Shred chicken; stir back into slow cooker. Roll up in tortillas; garnish as desired.

The easiest-ever way to cook egg noodles...bring water to a rolling boil, then turn off heat. Add noodles and let stand for 20 minutes, stirring twice. Perfect!

Chicken in the Garden

Makes 4 servings

2 T. olive oil
2 T. butter
4 boneless, skinless chicken
    breasts
1 onion, sliced
3 carrots, peeled and cut into
    2-inch pieces

10-3/4 oz. can cream of chicken
    soup
1 c. shredded Cheddar cheese
Optional: 1/2 c. sherry or
    Marsala wine
16-oz. pkg. frozen peas

Heat oil and butter in a pan until butter is melted. Add chicken
breasts; cook until golden and set aside. Place onion slices and
carrots in a slow cooker. Arrange chicken breasts on top of carrots; set
aside. Mix together soup, cheese and sherry or wine, if using; pour
over chicken mixture. Cover and cook on low setting for 6 hours. Add
frozen peas; mix well and continue to cook for an additional hour.

Enjoy hearty, comforting meals all winter long from your slow cooker...but don't put it away in the summertime! Cook up tender, mouthwatering sandwich fixin's and other summer favorites while the kitchen stays cool.

BBQ Chicken Sandwiches

Makes 8 to 10 servings

4 lbs. chicken
1-1/2 to 2 c. hickory smoke-
  flavored barbecue sauce

8 to 10 sandwich buns, split

Place chicken in a stockpot. Add water to cover and simmer until tender, about one hour. Drain chicken and cool; pull meat from bones. Place chicken in a slow cooker; cover with barbecue sauce. Cover and cook on high setting for 3 to 5 hours, stirring every 30 minutes. Chicken will shred during stirring. Serve on buns.

Whip up a speedy black bean salad. Combine one cup drained and rinsed black beans, 1/2 cup corn, 1/2 cup salsa and 1/4 teaspoon cumin or chili powder. Chill until serving time...tasty!

Chicken Mexi-Wraps

Makes 8 servings

3 boneless, skinless chicken
  breasts
1/2 c. salsa
8 10-inch flour tortillas,
  warmed

1 c. shredded Cheddar or
  Monterey Jack cheese
Garnish: shredded lettuce,
  chopped tomatoes, sour
  cream

Place chicken in a slow cooker; top with salsa. Cover and cook on
low setting for 6 to 8 hours. Remove chicken from slow cooker;
shred with a fork. Stir chicken back into juices in slow cooker. Spoon
chicken into warmed tortillas. Top with cheese and garnish as desired;
roll up.

A quick go-with for a slow-cooker meal...toss steamed
green beans, broccoli or zucchini with a little olive oil
and chopped fresh herbs.

Garlic & Tomato Chicken

Makes 4 to 6 servings

1 lb. boneless, skinless chicken
   breasts
2 15-oz. cans diced tomatoes
1 onion, chopped
1 clove garlic, minced

1 T. dried basil
salt and pepper to taste
1-1/4 c. water
cooked rotini pasta

Place chicken breasts in a slow cooker. Mix together remaining ingredients except rotini and pour over chicken. Cover and cook on low setting for 6 to 8 hours. Shred chicken with a fork; stir back into mixture in slow cooker. Serve over rotini.

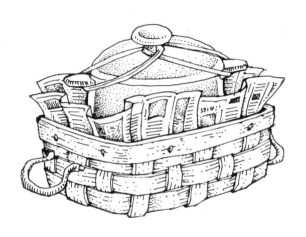

Toting soup in a slow cooker to keep it warm? Slip a large
rubber band under one handle, twist it around the
knob on the lid and secure on the other handle.

Slow-Cooker Chicken with Rice   *Makes 4 servings*

4 boneless, skinless chicken
    breasts
1/4 t. salt
1/4 t. pepper
1/4 t. paprika
1 T. oil
14-1/2 oz. can crushed
    tomatoes

1 red pepper, chopped
1 onion, chopped
1 clove garlic, minced
1/2 t. dried rosemary
10-oz. pkg. frozen peas
cooked rice

Sprinkle chicken with seasonings; set aside. Heat oil in a medium skillet over medium-high heat; add chicken and cook until golden on both sides. Arrange chicken in a slow cooker. In a small bowl, combine remaining ingredients except peas and rice; pour over chicken. Cover and cook on low setting for 7 to 9 hours, or on high setting for 3 to 4 hours. One hour before serving, stir in peas. Serve over rice.

Dress up stemmed water glasses...tie on a colorful blossom
or herb sprig with festive ribbon or raffia.

Just Peachy Chicken

Makes 4 servings

4 boneless, skinless chicken
    thighs
2 sweet potatoes, peeled and
    cubed

1 onion, chopped
2 T. cold water
3 T. cornstarch
1/2 c. peach preserves

Place chicken in a slow cooker; add sweet potatoes and onion. Cover and cook on low setting for 7 to 8 hours. Pour off juices from slow cooker into a large bowl; set aside. Cover chicken, sweet potatoes and onion to keep warm. In a heavy saucepan, combine water and cornstarch; mix well. Add reserved juices from slow cooker; stir in preserves. Cook and stir over medium heat, stirring frequently, until mixture boils and thickens. Simmer for 2 minutes; pour over chicken and vegetables.

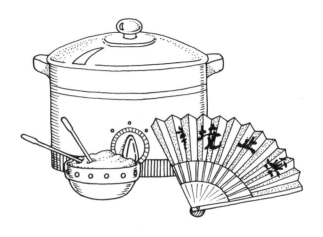

It's easy to separate frozen vegetables...put them in a colander and pour on hot water. Let water drain into the sink and add veggies to slow-cooker ingredients.

Asian Chicken

Makes 6 to 8 servings

3-1/2 lbs. boneless, skinless
   chicken breasts
1/3 c. peanut butter
2 T. soy sauce

3 T. orange juice
1/8 t. pepper
cooked rice or noodles

Place chicken in a slow cooker. Combine remaining ingredients except rice or noodles in a slow cooker; spread over chicken. Cover and cook on low setting for 6 to 8 hours, until chicken is tender. Serve with cooked rice or noodles.

The long, sweet hours that bring us all things good.
-Alfred, Lord Tennyson

Chicken Swiss Supreme

Makes 6 servings

3 slices bacon, crisply cooked, crumbled and drippings reserved
6 boneless, skinless chicken breasts

4-oz. can sliced mushrooms, drained
10-3/4 oz. can cream of chicken soup
1/2 c. Swiss cheese, diced

In a skillet over medium heat, cook chicken in reserved bacon drippings for 3 to 5 minutes, until lightly golden, turning once. Place chicken in a slow cooker; top with mushrooms. Stir soup into skillet; heat through and pour over chicken. Cover and cook on low setting for 4 to 5 hours, until chicken is cooked through. Top chicken with cheese and sprinkle with bacon. Cover and cook on high setting for 10 to 15 minutes, or until cheese is melted.

Keep canned beans on hand for quick and tasty pantry meals like chili, cold salads and hot side dishes. With lots of varieties to choose from, meals are never boring!

Nacho Chicken & Rice

Makes 4 to 6 servings

1 lb. boneless, skinless chicken
   breasts, cubed
2 10-3/4 oz. cans Cheddar
   cheese soup

1-1/4 c. water
16-oz. jar chunky salsa
1-1/4 c. long-cooking rice,
   uncooked

Combine all ingredients in a slow cooker. Cover and cook on low
setting for about 5 hours, or until chicken and rice are tender.

Purchasing a new slow cooker? Look for one that has a "warm" setting....it's perfect for keeping dips toasty through potlucks and parties.

Chicken-Chili Con Queso Dip

Makes 12 servings

2 boneless, skinless chicken breasts, cooked and shredded
32-oz. pkg. pasteurized process cheese spread, cubed
8-oz. pkg. cream cheese, cubed
16-oz. jar salsa
4-oz. can diced green chiles
tortilla chips

Combine all ingredients except tortilla chips in a slow cooker. Cover and cook on high setting for 1-1/2 to 2 hours, until cheese is melted, stirring occasionally. Reduce to low setting to serve. Serve with tortilla chips.

Tote your slow-cooker appetizers to the game-day tailgating party. Keep hot foods hot by picking up a power inverter that will use your car battery to power appliances.

Honey Chicken Wings

Makes 2-1/2 dozen

3 lbs. chicken wings
salt and pepper
2 c. honey
1 c. soy sauce

1/2 c. catsup
1/4 c. oil
2 cloves garlic, minced

Sprinkle wings with salt and pepper. Arrange on a broiler pan; broil 4 to 5 inches from heat until golden, about 10 minutes per side. Transfer wings to a slow cooker and set aside. Combine remaining ingredients in a small bowl; pour over wings. Cover and cook on low setting for 4 to 5 hours, or on high setting for 2 to 2-1/2 hours.

Be creative! Change flavors simply by substituting a different cooking liquid. Try your favorite cream soup or replace water with seasoned broth...just be sure to add the same amount.

7-Spice Sticky Chicken

Serves 4 to 6

3-lb. roasting chicken
4 t. salt
2 t. paprika
1 t. cayenne pepper
1 t. onion powder

1 t. dried thyme
1 t. white pepper
1/2 t. pepper
1/2 t. garlic powder
1 c. onion, chopped

Pat chicken dry inside and out with paper towels; set aside. Combine spices in a small bowl; mix well. Rub spice mixture well into chicken, inside and out. Place chicken in a large resealable zipping bag and refrigerate overnight. In the morning, place chicken in a slow cooker; top with chopped onion. Cover and cook on low setting for 8 to 10 hours.

All-day slow cooking works wonders on inexpensive, less-tender cuts of beef...arm and chuck roast, rump roast, short ribs, round steak and stew beef cook up juicy and delicious.

Mom's Fall-Apart Sunday Roast *Makes 6 servings*

3-lb. boneless beef chuck roast
salt, pepper and garlic powder
    to taste
1 to 2 T. oil
4 to 6 potatoes, peeled and
    quartered

1 to 2 onions, quartered
3 to 4 carrots, peeled and cut
    into chunks
3 14-1/2 oz. cans green beans,
    drained and liquid reserved

Sprinkle roast generously with salt, pepper and garlic powder. Heat oil
in a skillet; brown roast on all sides. Place potatoes in a slow cooker;
place roast on top of potatoes. Add onions, carrots and green beans,
sprinkling to taste with additional salt, pepper and garlic powder. Add
enough of reserved liquid from beans to cover ingredients about
halfway. Cover and cook on low setting for 6 to 8 hours.

Before placing in a slow cooker, sprinkle beef with this simple seasoning. Combine one cup salt, 1/4 cup pepper and 1/4 cup garlic powder. Mix all together and store in an airtight container for up to 6 months.

Fix & Go Swiss Steak

Makes 4 servings

1-1/2 lbs. boneless beef round
    steak, cut into serving-size
    pieces
1-1/2 oz. pkg. onion soup mix

2 14-1/2 oz. cans diced
    tomatoes
cooked rice

Arrange steak in a slow cooker; sprinkle with soup mix. Pour diced tomatoes over top. Cover and cook on high setting for 4 hours. Serve over rice.

Blend minced garlic, flavored cream cheese or shredded cheese
into warm mashed potatoes for a delicious side dish.

Magic Meatloaf

2 lbs. ground beef
2 eggs, beaten
1 c. quick-cooking oats,
   uncooked

1/2 c. catsup
1-1/2 c. mild salsa

Combine all ingredients and mix well. Shape into a loaf. Place in a slow cooker. Cover and cook on low setting for 8 to 10 hours, or on high setting for 4 to 6 hours.

Root vegetables like potatoes, carrots and onions grow tender
and sweet with all-day slow cooking. Give sweet potatoes
and parsnips a try too...delicious!

No-Peek Stew

Makes 4 to 6 servings

6 carrots, peeled and thickly
 sliced
3 potatoes, peeled and cubed
1 onion, sliced
3 stalks celery, sliced into
 1-inch pieces
2 lbs. stew beef, cubed
1/4 c. all-purpose flour
1 T. sugar
1 T. salt
1/4 t. pepper
14-oz. can tomato sauce

Arrange vegetables in a slow cooker, top with beef cubes. Blend flour, sugar, salt and pepper; sprinkle over meat. Pour tomato sauce over top; cover and cook on low setting for 8 to 9 hours.

To brown or not to brown? If you like, toss meat with all-purpose flour and brown with a little oil. It isn't really necessary, though! The exception is ground meat... browning eliminates excess grease.

Sandra's Slow-Cooker Brisket

Makes 6 servings

1 onion, sliced
3 to 4-lb. beef brisket
1 T. smoke-flavored cooking
   sauce

12-oz. bottle chili sauce
salt and pepper to taste

Arrange onion slices in a slow cooker; place brisket on top of onion. Add smoke-flavored cooking sauce; pour chili sauce over brisket. Sprinkle with salt and pepper. Cover and cook on low setting for 10 to 12 hours.

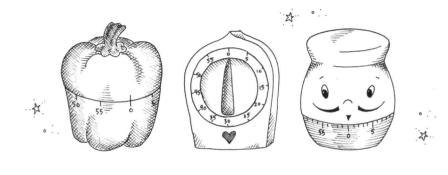

The feeling of friendship is like that of being comfortably filled with roast beef.

–Samuel Johnson

Beef Tips & Gravy

Makes 6 to 8 servings

3 lbs. stew beef, cubed
15-oz. can tomato sauce
2 c. water
1.35-oz. pkg. onion soup mix

1/3 c. instant tapioca, uncooked
1 to 2 t. beef bouillon granules
cooked egg noodles

Place beef in a slow cooker. Combine remaining ingredients except noodles; pour over beef. Cover and cook on low setting for 8 to 10 hours, or on high setting for 5 to 6 hours. Serve over cooked noodles.

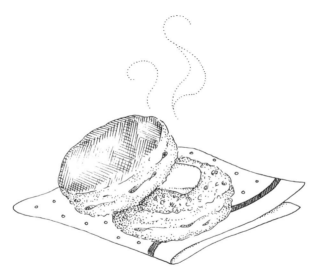

Fluffy hot biscuits are a must with stew! Add a personal touch to refrigerated biscuits...brush with butter, then sprinkle with dried herbs, coarse salt or sesame seed before baking.

Country-Style Beef Stew

Makes 4 to 6 servings

2 lbs. stew beef, cubed
1/4 c. all-purpose flour
1/2 t. pepper
2 T. Worcestershire sauce
5 potatoes, peeled and cubed

5 carrots, peeled and diced
1 stalk celery, diced
1/4 c. onion, diced
1-1/2 c. beef broth
1 c. peas

Place stew meat in a slow cooker. Mix flour with pepper and sprinkle over meat; stir to coat. Add remaining ingredients except peas; mix well. Cover and cook on low setting for 10 to 12 hours, or on high setting for 5 to 6 hours. Stir in peas 30 minutes before serving.

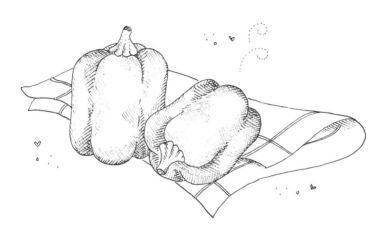

Slice & dice meats and veggies ahead of time and refrigerate
in separate plastic zipping bags. In the morning, toss everything
into the slow cooker and you're on your way.

Homestyle Stuffed Peppers

Makes 4 servings

1-1/2 lbs. ground beef
1 onion, finely chopped
1 c. long-cooking rice,
    uncooked

4 green peppers, tops removed
15-oz. can tomato sauce
Optional: salt-free herb
    seasoning to taste

Mix together ground beef, onion and rice; spoon into peppers.
Arrange peppers in a slow cooker; pour tomato sauce over top.
Sprinkle with seasoning, if desired. Cover and cook on low setting
for 5 to 6 hours.

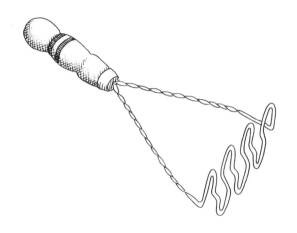

An easy way to crumble ground beef...use a potato masher.
It makes browning so quick & easy.

Slow-Cooker Taco Soup

Makes 8 to 10 servings

1 lb. ground beef
1 onion, diced
1 clove garlic, minced
12-oz. bottle green taco sauce
4-oz. can green chiles
2 to 3 15-oz. cans black beans,
    drained and rinsed

15-1/4 oz. can corn, drained
15-oz. can tomato sauce
2 c. water
1-1/4 oz. pkg. taco seasoning
    mix
Garnish: sour cream, shredded
    Cheddar cheese, corn chips

Brown beef, onion and garlic in a large skillet over medium heat;
drain. In a slow cooker, combine beef mixture and remaining
ingredients except garnish. Cover and cook on high setting for
one hour. Serve with sour cream, shredded cheese and corn chips.

Put on a savory soup to cook in your slow cooker, then enjoy winter fun with your family. After a snow hike or ice skating, a hot, delicious dinner will be waiting for you...what could be cozier?

Santa Fe Corn & Bean Soup

Makes 6 to 8 servings

1 lb. ground beef
1/2 onion, diced
2 10-oz. can tomatoes with
   chiles
2 c. water
16-oz. can kidney beans
16-oz. can pinto beans

16-oz. can black beans
11-oz. can corn
1-oz. pkg. ranch salad
   dressing mix
1-1/4 oz. pkg. taco seasoning
   mix

Brown beef and onion together in a skillet; drain. Transfer to a
slow cooker; mix in remaining ingredients. Cover and cook on low
setting for 6 to 8 hours, or on high setting for 3 to 4 hours, until
heated through.

Have some fun with chili toppers! Instead of crackers, try diced tomatoes, sliced jalapeño peppers, a big dollop of sour cream or creamy ranch dressing...don't forget crushed tortilla chips for crunch!

Texas Beef Chili

Makes 6 servings

2 lbs. stew beef, cubed
1 onion, chopped
15-oz. can chunky tomato
    sauce

12-oz. jar thick and chunky
    salsa
1 green pepper, chopped

Combine all ingredients except green pepper in a slow cooker. Cover and cook on low setting for 8 to 10 hours. Stir in pepper; increase to high setting and cook for an additional 15 to 20 minutes.

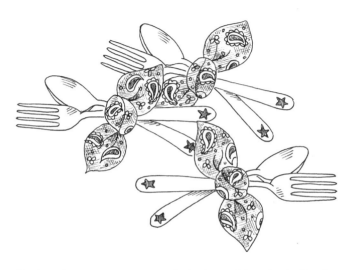

Colorful bandannas make great picnic napkins...look for inexpensive
ones in all kinds of fun prints at your local craft store.

Honey-Mustard Short Ribs

Makes 4 servings

3 to 4 lbs. bone-in beef short
   ribs
salt and pepper to taste
1 c. hickory smoke-flavored
   barbecue sauce

3 T. honey
1 T. Dijon mustard
3 cloves garlic, minced
2 T. cornstarch
2 T. cold water

Sprinkle ribs with salt and pepper; place in a slow cooker and set aside. Combine barbecue sauce, honey, mustard, garlic and additional salt and pepper, if desired; pour over ribs. Cover and cook on low setting for 6 to 7 hours. During the last 30 minutes of cooking, whisk cornstarch into water; add to slow cooker, stirring until thickened.

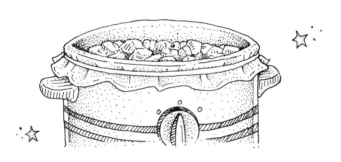

For easy slow-cooker clean-up, spray it with non-stick vegetable spray before filling. Even easier...use a toss-away plastic liner.

Lone Star BBQ Ribs

Makes 4 to 6 servings

3 lbs. bone-in beef short ribs
1 c. water
1/2 c. barbecue sauce

1/2 c. dry red wine or beef
  broth
1 T. Worcestershire sauce

Arrange ribs in a slow cooker. Mix remaining ingredients together and pour over ribs. Cover and cook on low setting for 8 to 10 hours.

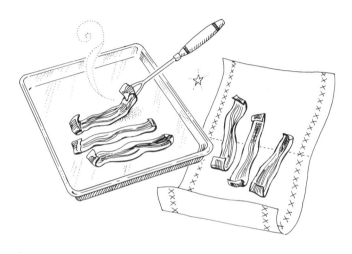

Here's a quick tip for bacon. Arrange slices on a baking sheet and bake at 350 degrees. It'll be crispy in about 15 minutes...no messy spatters!

BBQ Cowboy Beans

Makes 8 servings

1/2 lb. ground beef, browned
   and drained
6 to 8 slices bacon, crisply
   cooked and crumbled
15-oz. can lima beans
15-oz. can kidney beans

16-oz. can pork & beans
1/2 c. barbecue sauce
1/2 c. sugar
1/2 c. brown sugar, packed
1 t. smoke-flavored cooking
   sauce

Combine all ingredients in a slow cooker; stir thoroughly. Cover and cook on low setting for 3 to 4 hours.

Rolls and buns will drip less when filled with juicy
slow-cooked meat if they're toasted first.

Smokey BBQ Beef Rolls

Makes 16 servings

4 to 6-lb. beef brisket
1 T. onion salt
1 T. celery salt
1 t. garlic salt
coarse pepper to taste

1/4 c. smoke-flavored cooking
   sauce
1/4 c. Worcestershire sauce
16 rolls, split

Rub brisket with salts and pepper; place in slow cooker. Stir sauces together; gently pour over roast. Cover; cook on low setting for 8 to 10 hours. Slice or shred meat; serve on rolls.

Slow down and enjoy life.
-Eddie Cantor

Diner-Style Burgers

Makes 8 servings

2 lbs. ground beef
1 egg, beaten
1 c. onion, finely chopped
1/2 c. shredded Cheddar cheese
2 T. catsup
2 T. evaporated milk

1/2 c. cracker crumbs
salt and pepper to taste
1 c. all-purpose flour
2 to 3 T. oil
10-3/4 oz. can cream of
　mushroom soup

Mix together ground beef, egg, onion, cheese, catsup, milk, cracker crumbs, salt and pepper. Shape into 8 patties; roll in flour. Heat oil in a large skillet over medium heat; brown patties. Arrange patties in a slow cooker alternately with soup. Cover and cook on high setting for 3 to 4 hours.

Need to add a little zing to a soup or stew? Just add a splash of Worcestershire sauce, lemon juice or flavored vinegar.

Beef Barley Soup

Makes 4 to 6 servings

2 c. carrots, peeled and thinly
    sliced
1 c. celery, thinly sliced
3/4 c. green pepper, diced
1 c. onion, diced
1 lb. stew beef, cubed
1/2 c. pearl barley, uncooked

1/4 c. fresh parsley, chopped
3 cubes beef bouillon
2 T. catsup
1 t. salt
3/4 t. dried basil
5 c. water

Layer vegetables, beef and barley in a slow cooker; add seasonings.
Pour water over all; do not stir. Cover and cook on low setting for 9 to
11 hours.

A garden-fresh side dish that's ready in a jiffy. Stir together
one cup sour cream, 2 tablespoons vinegar and 4 tablespoons
sugar. Fold in two peeled and thinly sliced cucumbers;
add salt and pepper to taste.

Bar-B-Q Steak Sandwiches   *Makes 12 to 14 servings*

3 lbs. boneless beef round
   steak, cut into several large
   pieces
2 onions, chopped
3/4 c. celery, thinly sliced
1/2 c. catsup
1/2 to 3/4 c. water
1/3 c. lemon juice
1/3 c. Worcestershire sauce

3 T. brown sugar, packed
3 T. cider vinegar
2 t. mustard
1 t. chili powder
1/2 t. hot pepper sauce
1/2 t. paprika
2 t. salt
1 t. pepper
12 to 14 hamburger buns, split

Place meat, onions and celery in a slow cooker; set aside. Combine remaining ingredients except buns in a bowl. Stir and pour over meat. Cover and cook for 6 to 8 hours, until meat is tender. Remove meat and cool slightly; shred with a fork and return to sauce in slow cooker. Heat through and serve on buns.

Feeding a crowd is a breeze with a slow cooker. Fill it with shredded meat, burgers or meatballs, set out bakery-fresh rolls, chips and coleslaw...and you're ready to just let guests help themselves!

Shredded Beef Sandwiches   *Makes 10 to 12 servings*

12-oz. jar sliced pepperoncini
4-lb. beef chuck roast
1-3/4 t. dried basil
1-1/2 t. dried oregano
1-1/2 t. garlic powder
1-1/4 t. salt

1/4 t. pepper
1/4 c. water
1 onion, sliced
10 to 12 sandwich buns, split
   and toasted

Pour pepperoncini with liquid into a slow cooker; add roast. Mix together spices, salt and pepper; sprinkle over meat. Add water and onion. Cover and cook on low setting for 8 to 9 hours, until meat is tender. Remove roast; shred using 2 forks. Return meat to slow cooker; mix well. Using a slotted spoon, place meat on buns.

Slow cookers come in all sizes, so why not have a couple on hand?
A large-size slow cooker is ideal for family-size roasts, while a
smaller size is just right for a savory appetizer dip or fondue.

Italian Pot Roast

Makes 4 to 6 servings

2 to 3-lb. beef chuck roast
1 T. oil
2 14-1/2 oz. cans Italian-style
   stewed tomatoes

4-oz. can sliced mushrooms,
   drained
Optional: cooked egg noodles or
   mashed potatoes

In a skillet over medium heat, brown roast in oil on both sides. Place
roast in a slow cooker; pour tomatoes over top. Cover and cook on
low setting for 10 to 11 hours. About 15 minutes before serving, stir
in mushrooms; cover and heat through. If desired, serve with cooked
egg noodles or potatoes.

Check the liquid in the slow cooker about 30 minutes before done cooking. If it seems too juicy, just remove the lid and turn the setting up to high...excess liquid will evaporate.

Spicy Tortellini & Meatballs   *Makes 6 to 8 servings*

14-oz. pkg. frozen cooked
   Italian meatballs, thawed
16-oz. pkg. frozen broccoli,
   cauliflower and carrot blend,
   thawed
2 c. cheese tortellini, uncooked

2 10-3/4 oz. cans cream of
   mushroom soup
2-1/4 c. water
1/2 to 1 t. ground cumin
salt and pepper to taste

Combine meatballs, vegetables and tortellini in a slow cooker. In a
large bowl, whisk together soup, water and seasonings. Pour over
meatball mixture; stir to combine well. Cover and cook on low setting
for 3 to 4 hours.

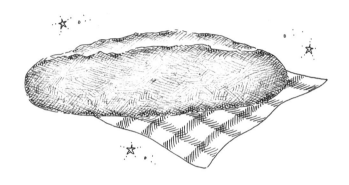

For flavorful, fast-fix bread to serve with Spaghetti
& Meatballs, simply brush Italian bread slices with butter.
Sprinkle on garlic & herb seasoning blend and broil until golden.

Spaghetti & Meatballs

Makes 4 to 6 servings

1 lb. frozen cooked meatballs,
    thawed
26-oz. jar spaghetti sauce
1 onion, chopped
1-1/2 c. water

8-oz. pkg. spaghetti, uncooked
    and broken into 3-inch
    pieces
Garnish: grated Parmesan
    cheese

Combine meatballs, spaghetti sauce, onion and water in a slow
cooker. Cover and cook on low setting for 6 to 8 hours. Stir well;
add broken spaghetti. Increase to high setting; cover and cook for
an additional hour, stirring once during cooking. Serve sprinkled with
Parmesan cheese.

To get the best results when cooking in a slow cooker, be sure ingredients fill the crock at least 1/2 full and no more than 2/3 full.

Zesty Italian Hoagies

Makes 8 servings

3 to 4-lb. beef rump roast
8-oz. bottle Italian salad
    dressing

12-oz. jar pepperoncini, drained
8 hoagie buns, split

Place roast in a slow cooker. Pour salad dressing over roast and arrange pepperoncini on top. Cover and cook on low setting for 8 to 10 hours. Remove roast from slow cooker and shred with a fork. Return to slow cooker; mix with pepperoncini and spoon onto buns.

Stir in a little quick-cooking tapioca with other ingredients
for a roast or stew...broth will thicken magically as it cooks!

Farmhouse Pot Roast

3-lb. beef chuck roast
4-oz. can sliced mushrooms,
   drained
8 redskin potatoes, cubed
1/2 lb. baby carrots

3 stalks celery, chopped
14-1/2 oz. can beef broth
2 c. water
26-oz. can cream of mushroom
   soup

Place roast in a slow cooker; top with vegetables. In a medium bowl, blend together broth, water and soup; pour over roast. Cover and cook on low setting for 6 to 8 hours, until roast is very tender.

Flour tortillas are tastiest when warmed. Stack tortillas between moistened paper towels and microwave on high setting for 20 to 30 seconds...easy!

Fiesta Beef Fajitas

Makes 4 to 6 servings

2 lbs. beef skirt or flank steak
14-1/2 oz. can tomatoes with
   chiles
2 1-1/4 oz. pkgs. fajita
   seasoning mix
1 green pepper, coarsely
   chopped

1 onion, coarsely chopped
8 to 12 10-inch flour tortillas,
   warmed
Garnish: guacamole, sour
   cream, shredded Cheddar
   cheese, salsa

Place meat in a slow cooker and set aside. Mix tomatoes with chiles and fajita seasoning together in a bowl; pour over meat. Cover and cook on high setting for 4 hours; reduce to low and cook for an additional 2 hours. Add green pepper and onion; cover and continue cooking on low setting for an additional hour. Shred meat; serve on warmed tortillas with desired garnishes.

Roast beef sandwiches from the slow cooker are so deliciously juicy! To keep that juice from dripping, wrap individual servings in aluminum foil, then peel back as they're eaten.

Savory Roast Sandwiches
Makes 10 to 12 servings

3 to 4-lb. beef chuck roast
14-oz. bottle catsup
1/2 c. taco sauce
1 onion, chopped
2 cloves garlic, pressed
2 T. brown sugar, packed

2 T. Worcestershire sauce
1 T. vinegar
1/8 t. dried oregano
1/8 t. dry mustard
1/8 t. pepper
10 to 12 hard rolls, split

Place roast in a slow cooker; set aside. Mix together remaining ingredients except rolls; pour over roast. Cover and cook on low setting for 5 to 6 hours. Remove roast from slow cooker; shred with 2 forks. Return shredded meat to slow cooker; heat through and serve on rolls.

Dress up glasses of lemonade or iced tea by dipping the
rims into lemon juice, then into sparkling sugar.

Aunt B's Sloppy Joes

Makes 10 servings

3 lbs. ground beef
1 c. onion, chopped
1 c. green pepper, chopped
2 cloves garlic, chopped
1-1/2 c. catsup
1/2 c. water

1/4 c. mustard
1/4 c. cider vinegar
1/4 c. Worcestershire sauce
1 T. chili powder
10 whole-wheat hamburger
    buns, split

In a skillet over medium heat, cook ground beef, onion, green pepper and garlic until browned and tender; drain. Combine in a slow cooker with remaining ingredients except buns. Cover and cook on low setting for 6 to 8 hours, or on high setting for 3 to 4 hours. Spoon into buns.

Soft veggies like peas and spinach don't need to cook all day.
Stir them into the slow cooker in the last 30 minutes...they'll
keep their fresh color and firm texture better.

Slow-Cooker Pizza

Makes 8 to 10 servings

1/2 lb. ground beef
1 onion, chopped
8-oz. jar spaghetti sauce
16-oz. jar pizza sauce
12-oz. pkg. kluski egg noodles, cooked

8-oz. pkg. sliced pepperoni
8-oz. pkg. shredded mozzarella cheese
8-oz. pkg. shredded Cheddar cheese

Brown ground beef and onion in a large skillet over medium heat; drain. Stir in sauces; simmer until heated through. Layer half the noodles in a slow cooker and top with half each of meat sauce, pepperoni and cheeses. Repeat layering. Cover and cook on low setting for one hour, or on high setting for 30 minutes, until cheese is melted.

Slow cookers are perfect party helpers! Just plug
them in and they'll keep appetizers bubbly,
hot and yummy with no effort at all.

Swedish Meatballs

Makes 6 servings

1 lb. ground beef
1 onion, chopped
6 graham crackers, finely
   crushed
1 T. sugar

1 t. salt
1/2 t. pepper
3 to 4 t. milk
10-1/2 oz. can beef broth

Combine all ingredients except broth in a large bowl. Mix well, adding a little extra milk if mixture appears too dry. Form into one-inch balls. Cook meatballs in a lightly greased skillet over medium heat until lightly browned, turning frequently. Remove meatballs from skillet; arrange in a slow cooker and set aside. Add broth to drippings in skillet; cook and stir over medium heat until slightly thickened. Pour broth mixture over meatballs; cover and cook on high setting for one hour.

Make it a meal. Spoon South-of-the-Border Dip over wedges
of warm cornbread and serve with a chopped salad of
tomatoes and lettuce...a speedy supper!

South-of-the-Border Dip

Makes 2-1/2 dozen

1 lb. ground beef
1 lb. ground pork sausage
16-oz. pkg. Mexican
   pasteurized process
   cheese spread, cubed

10-3/4 oz. can cream of
   mushroom soup
4-oz. can chopped green chiles
tortilla chips

Brown ground beef and sausage in a skillet; drain. Combine with cheese, soup and chiles in a slow cooker. Cover and cook on low setting for 3 to 4 hours, until cheese is melted. Serve with tortilla chips. Makes 7 to 8 cups.

A covered slow cooker cooks with little or no evaporation...
all the delicious cooking juices combine to create a scrumptious
gravy. Just add the amount of liquid that the recipe calls for.

Teriyaki Beef

Makes 4 servings

1/3 c. teriyaki marinade
8-oz. can crushed pineapple
1-1/2 lb. boneless beef
   chuck steak

Optional: cooked rice

Spray a slow cooker with non-stick vegetable spray; add marinade and pineapple with juice. Place steak in marinade mixture. Cover and cook on high setting for 2-1/2 to 3-1/2 hours. If desired, serve over cooked rice.

CHICKEN INDEX

BEEF INDEX

Our Story

Back in 1984, we were next-door neighbors raising our families in the little town of Delaware, Ohio. Two moms with small children, we were looking for a way to do what we loved and stay home with the kids too. We had always shared a love of home cooking and making memories with family & friends and so, after many a conversation over the backyard fence, **Gooseberry Patch** was born.

We put together our first catalog at our kitchen tables, enlisting the help of our loved ones wherever we could. From that very first mailing, we found an immediate connection with many of our customers and it wasn't long before we began receiving letters, photos and recipes from these new friends. In 1992, we put together our very first cookbook, compiled from hundreds of these recipes and, the rest, as they say, is history.

Hard to believe it's been over 25 years since those kitchen-table days! From that original little **Gooseberry Patch** family, we've grown to include an amazing group of creative folks who love cooking, decorating and creating as much as we do. Today, we're best known for our homestyle, family-friendly cookbooks, now recognized as national bestsellers.

One thing's for sure, we couldn't have done it without our friends all across the country. Each year, we're honored to turn thousands of your recipes into our collectible cookbooks. Our hope is that each book captures the stories and heart of all   you who have shared with us. Whether you've been with us since the beginning or are just discovering us, welcome to the **Gooseberry Patch** family!

Vickie & JoAnn

Want to hear the latest from **Gooseberry Patch**?
www.gooseberrypatch.com

Join
Our Circle of
Friends

You Tube

Read Our Blog

Find us on Facebook

Follow us on twitter

1·800·854·6673